Coronation Season

Lakeya Brown

Copyright © 2024 Lakeya Brown

All rights reserved. No part of this publication may be reproduced, distributed, or transmitted in any form without the prior written permission of the author, except in the case of brief quotations embodied in reviews and certain other noncommercial uses permitted by copyright law.

Dedication

To the chosen ones: Allow the pruning as many times as necessary in order to grow in purpose.

TABLE OF CONTENTS

THE AWAKENING

It is Well	1
The Awakening	2
A Letter of Apology and Gratitude	3
Deserving Of	4
Envy	5
Now	6
Fear and Love	7
Certain	8
Palatable	9
Faith	10
I Know Who I Am	11
Unearthed Greatness	12
Your Soul	13
Time and Season	14
How Many	15
Gleaming Light	16
Ready	17
Speak Your Truth	18
No Rescue Needed	19
Doors Open	20
The Unveiling	21
Love's True Identity	22
Mundane	23
Questions	24
Relinquish	25
Life	26
Lesson in Discomfort	27
Progress	28

Stillness	29
Beware	30
Exactly Enough	31
Life's a Journey	32
Renewed Wings	33
God Exists	34
Starting Over	35
The Truth	36
Grief	37
Thoughts	38
New Light	39
Accepted and Adored	40

THE PURIFICATION

The Decree	41
Stillness	42
Surrender	43
Power of Forgiveness	44
Blossoms Amidst Ruin	45
The Alchemy	46
Peace	47
Famine	48
Sugar Coated Egos	49
Renewal	50
Canvas	51
How to Move	52
New Season	53
Chosen Ones	54
Rise	55
Flame	56
Diamond	57
Worth	58

Trailblazer	59
River	60
Force	61
Grace	62
Voices	63
Human Spirit	64
Boldly	65
Pause	66
Comparison	67
Fire	68
Patience	69
Anomaly	70

THE HEALING

Healing	71
The Journey Within	72
Self- discovery	73
Emerging	74
Gratitude	75
A Time of Laughter	76
Perspective	77
Pure and Beautiful	78
The Strength of Foundations	79
Growth	80
Be Well	81
Strength	82
Self-love	83
The Healing Woman	84
The Heart of a Fighter	85
A Father's Love	86
Mending	87
Light Bearer	88

Faith	89
Empowered	90
Mastering Letting Go	91
Dreams	92
Exposure	93
Passion	94
You Can	95
Fill Your Cup	96
The Beauty of Change	97
Choose	98
Freedom	99
Only a Lesson	100
Legacy	101
Connection	102
Humility	103
Incredible Rebirth	104
Gentleness	105
In Your Presence	106

THE CROWNING

The Coronation	107
Seasons Change	108
The Weight of the Crown	109
Eternal Seeds of Resilience	110
Leaving to Receive	111
King and Queens Flight	112
Crown of Beauty	113
Noble Character	114
A Queen's King	115
Wisdom	116
Determination	117
Will You?	118
Boundless Visionary	119
You	120

Messy Grace	121
Hero	122
Strength Applauded	123
Perfect Pace	124
Simplicity	125
Free	126
Letting Yourself Feel It	127
Imperfections	128
Energy	129
Calm	130
The Gift	131
Queen's Play	132
Wealth Within	133
To Heal	134
Such a Time as This	135
Empathy	136
Remember Who You Are	137
Mirror, Mirror	138
Unshaken	139
Qualities	140
Create	141
Unfinished Dreams	142
The Courage to Crossover	143
Clothed in Strength	144
Seasons Change	145
The Fruit of Possibilities	146
Simply Being	147
Battlefield	148
Symphony	149
You Are Still Becoming	150

The Awakening

It is Well

Waters from the storehouse of heaven
flow to and through my soul.
The years of watering others and neglecting myself
have caused a burden that I cannot lift on my own.
I need to be refreshed and restored.
I can't tell the grit from the bruising
or separate the wound from the roughness.
I'm thirsty for what self-care cannot repair alone.
So, I steal away to a place of stillness and solitude.
A place that is both physical and internal.
Rebuilding the ruined walls of my boundaries,
repairing the breaches of my heart.
Resting until I have become refreshed
for the journey that lies ahead.
I've finally arrived at the place
where it is well.

The Awakening

Light breaks through the dark,
Silent whispers stir the soul,
Awake, the heart blooms.

Coronation Season

A Letter of Apology and Gratitude

Dear Me,

I owe you an apology, an honest and heartfelt one, for the times I've given your time, energy, and presence freely to others, and neglected your needs. I regret nothing because it taught me a valuable lesson. It challenged me to elevate myself. I apologize because I need to heal and forgive myself for what I didn't understand. I apologize for every time I left your heart vulnerable and unguarded.

I apologize for not holding firm boundaries and for letting your throne be shaken and your crown slip and tarnish. You deserved protection, respect, and to be loved purely and fiercely. Today, as I self-explore and reflect, I want to express my deep gratitude to you. Thank you for your unwavering strength, for enduring through times of neglect and still shining brightly.

As I elevate to this new and higher version of myself, I promise that you will be cherished and loved. I promise to guard your heart and serve it with the care and purity it needs. I will hold boundaries, ensuring your throne remains unchallenged and your crown untarnished. I vow to forgive myself for past mistakes and nurture our bond with love and respect.

From this day forward, I will honor, protect, and cherish you. You are worthy of all the love you give and so much more. Together, we will walk this path, with our heart, throne, and crown held high.

With deepest love and respect,
Me

Deserving Of

You deserve to function in the way
you were created to.
To be strong and feminine, dainty and bold.
You deserve to lather yourself with
affirmations and self-care.

To guard your heart with all your might,
and forsake others' needs to tend to your own.
You deserve to heal, to be still
and slay dragons of doubt.

As you provide for others, a guiding light,
don't forget that you too follow the greatest Light.
Just because you carry it with grace,
doesn't mean it isn't heavy.
This journey of strength and depth calls out to you.
For this reason, are you ready?

In our hands, the generations take form.
With our words, dry bones live
and warriors are born.
An endless journey,
for the one who bears the crown.

Envy

In the glow of her light, they stand in awe,
an authentic soul, even with her flaws.
She walks with grace, timeless and regal.
A divine presence, she is beyond comparison.
Her heart, a beacon, pure and bright,
radiating love, an eternal light.
With every step and encounter,
she leaves a change, an imprint of light.
She is strength and adorned with boundless grace.
Even though shadows form from envious eyes,
her love cannot be dulled,
her love and pureness are strong.
Her spirit is free, refusing to be chained and caged
by jealous hearts, by souls choosing to be constrained.
She rises above, with wings unfurled,
taking flight, she soars,
Releasing sparks of love, joy,
and peace ready to be kindled.
In their envy, they seek to find
the secret to her peace of mind.
But she remains untouchable and protected.
For she is love, she is a timeless queen.

Now

Are you able to start now?
To commit your heart and your will
to embrace your journey of self-discovery.
To explore your inner workings
with love, compassion, and forgiveness.
To embrace your gifting
and cultivate it with seeds of resiliency.
Cease to resist the unleashing of potential.
Let yourself be wild & free.
Give yourself permission to commit,
to grow, and live a sacred life.

Fear and Love

Fear and love cannot occupy the same space.
Fear is like the wild jealous beast, willing to
compromise and cheat to quench its bloodlust.
Love is bold and wise as an eagle,
yet vicious enough to defend its rightful place.
Once you've tasted both fear and love,
you'll understand why the mind can
only offer space for one.
Fear condemns and exacerbates worry,
love offers freedom and provides empathy.
Your mind builds its house,
and where you sow your energy,
your life will follow.
Will you choose to live in a state of fear
or from a place of freedom?
Fear and love cannot occupy the same space.

Coronation Season

Certain

You were certain when you took
your meeting with God.
Assured and confident that for this moment
you were born.
Certainty has now turned to doubt.
Where there was once boldness,
the corrupted seeds of fear sprout.
Remember who you are.
Remember whose you are.

In your awakening, with all your love and strength,
let unshakeable faith lead you.
Ascend to hear your Father's heart and mind.
On your way up, etch the sun,
let the stars burn bright in memory,
as they dim in your presence.
For you were created in the image of your father.
Let the certainty of His voice
draw you forward in darkness as it would in the light.
Your strength and courage will become clear,
and darkness will flee in every direction.

Palatable

Not every lifestyle is the same,
for conformity is not our portion.
Be one of a courageous and holistic diet,
feeding your soul with truth and silence.

Eating things that you know to be pure and true,
living authentically, just as you were created to.
Not palatable to everyone,
embracing the freedom that comes from being undone.

In a world that craves conformity to fill the voids,
stand tall in your peculiarity,
for your quintessence is a unique blend,
accepted only by those with a palate
as sophisticated as yours or greater.

Do not succumb to forceful societal molds,
be bold, letting your spirit shine, fiercely and free.
Welcome the path less traveled,
live with pure-hearted intentions,
allowing your soul to fly.

For true beauty lies in being true,
choosing to live authentically, moment by moment.
Not every life is designed to be the same,
so be yourself, unapologetically.
Even if it means that you are unpalatable.

Faith

Faith is our lighthouse, furiously illuminating
within our very being.
She was created to guide you through thick and thin.
Even when it seems impossible,
radically believe in yourself, and let it show.
We each have the ability to save ourselves,
So lean into your discernment,
and your conviction will grow.
With every determined step, let faith awaken.
Let it shine and inspire others to believe,
causing fear to remain at bay.

I Know Who I Am

You want me to be more like you,
watered down and easily consumable,
so you can chew my bones and crush my soul
with the acidity of your hate and jealousy.

You want to slither freely down the walls of my garden,
Sowing seeds of deception and enmity,
Like your father in the beginning.
You want me to bend and conform,
to be remade into your image.

You want me to lessen my worth
and compromise, just as you did,
For the approval of those who depreciate
with every breath they release.

But I cannot.
I cannot forsake my position
or compromise my value.
I've awakened from my slumber.
I know who I am, and so do you.

Unearthed Greatness

There are no undo buttons
or easy paths in this life.
Everything and everyone is evolving.
Patterns repeat until you unlearn defeat.

We all begin as passengers
revolving around the sun,
until we realize we are greater.
Destined to command the sun,
to speak to the mountains,
to guide the winds,
and lull the waves.

We can unearth new levels of greatness,
or remain in mediocre bliss.
Whatever choices we make,
they are ours alone.
Free will, not fate.

I hope you'll choose greatness.
Release the pain that binds you to the past.
Come, walk yourself forward,
and join those who are free,
planting seeds of liberty
for ourselves and the generations to come.

Your Soul

Until it is reconciled to its Creator,
your soul will ache in unbearable ways.
It will feel as though you might drown in the pain.

You will use people, places, and things
to medicate the wounds.
You will crush yourself into pieces
and offer them freely to everyone you meet,
hoping to feel loved.
But such love is fleeting,
a momentary balm.

Once you've had your fill, you'll rebuild,
only to break yourself into finer shards.
You'll move your boundaries further back,
leaving your soul exposed.

Listen to your soul.
It wants to heal,
to help you find your way home.
Secure the palace of your heart,
uphold your boundaries,
and dwell within the walls of wholeness.

Time and Season

Slow down. Write it down.
When you consume too quickly,
you become reckless—
with your words,
with your process,
and with your time.

When you rush,
there is no simmering of flavor,
no time to mature.

Pause. Look around.
Stop and adjust.
Stop and give gratitude.
Take in the view
from a bird's-eye perspective.

When you rush, you miss
the season of clarity,
The moments to adjust and readjust,
to recalibrate and plan your next move.

Haste robs you of
awareness and greatness.

How Many

How many tiny miracles
have conspired to create this moment
for you to stand in dominion,
as the chosen creation you are?

You are fearfully and wonderfully made,
causing the stars to blush
at the brilliance of your light.

Embrace your beauty.
Let it flower and mature.
You are fearfully created.
This, you must know.

Gleaming Light

In the abyss of darkness and deferred dreams,
a light gleams.
The wild ones see it,
a growing inferno.

As you summon courage
to pass through shadows,
it shines brilliantly,
luring you like a moth to a flame.

Stomach churning, you walk
through the valley,
inhaling the stench of death and fear,
just to lay hold of
your purpose and dreams.

Ready

When you are ready,
every excuse will die.
This time, you'll bury them
without a desire to resurrect the dead.

Excuses abound for why we shouldn't heal.
Do not let fear intimidate you.
It takes courage from the depths of your being
to sidestep insecurities
and leap over every excuse.

A still spirit is needed
to hear the soft beckoning of your conscience.
Listen to your atoms calling your soul,
to the deep calling unto deep.

Wrap yourself in courage.
Grieve your own will,
and surrender to the depths of your soul.
Self-awareness is a rollercoaster,
but your surrender is necessary.

Will you go deeper?
Understand the value of peace,
and the weight of truth.

Speak Your Truth

There is no harm in speaking your truth.
It is the key ingredient of authenticity.

Perhaps your truth exposed their fangs,
unmasking frenemies,
revealing snakes slithering through your garden.

Maybe your radiance illuminates their fraud,
your organic living makes their façades tremble.
You're too bright;
your truth makes their wounds ache.

Though created for greatness,
they've learned to thrive in shadows.
But you?
You shine unapologetically.
There is no harm in speaking your truth.

No Rescue Needed

I've never needed rescuing.
Only those who believe in fairytales
long to be saved.

Even when my strength ran low,
I was still strong enough to rescue myself.
I've honed the art of surviving,
learning to fight when war is necessary,
to heal with the smallest of ingredients,
to release seasons that no longer serve me.

I've never needed rescuing,
only understanding.
To meet me, you must face yourself.
Strip away ego-driven expectations
and embrace my essence.

Doors Open

The doors that were shut are now open.
Run with power,
with zeal,
with fire in your heart.

As you run to the end of yourself,
angels assigned to your destiny
will lift you higher.

Run until your faith grows wings.
Run without fear.
This is your time.

The Unveiling

This is the unraveling of who you were
and the unveiling of
who you were always meant to be.

It is time for the gifts within you to mature.
Like precious gems,
I hid you.
From thieves, from insecurity,
from death itself.

You've been preserved for this moment.
This is your unveiling.
Step forward in the fullness of who you are.

Love's True Identity

It is in love's secure embrace
that we find solace.

If love is inconsistent in its intentions,
can it truly be pure?
If it offers no rest,
can it truly be true?

Perfect love casts out fear.
Providing a sanctuary,
a place to lay your burdens down,
a place to replenish joy.

True love wraps you in safety,
allowing you to release your cares
and breathe freely again.

Mundane

In the mundane and the chaos,
Life's treasures are unearthed.

Be present,
for in an instant,
we return to dust.

Cherish the morning blush
and the starlit skies.
Let simple conversations fill your cup.
Savor laughter's nectar,
consume it fully.

Leave nothing unsaid.
Touch everything with kindness.
We are but vapor,
here today,
gone tomorrow.

Live with childlike wonder
and limitless gratitude.

Questions

When did you stop asking, "Why?"
When did you trade wonder for safety?

Do you remember meeting curiosity?
When you trusted your gut
and built worlds unknown.

Curiosity unlocks the answers,
revealing parts of yourself
you've long forgotten.

Return to your childlike spirit.
Ask again.
Discover again.

Relinquish

I began to relinquish
the weight of unhealthy thoughts.
I unsubscribed from pain
and subscribed to peace.

I built a sanctuary of love,
a queendom of self-respect.
Gratitude became my cornerstone,
falling in love
one blessing at a time.

Life

Life is too short for shallow ties,
for hollow laughter,
for deceitful tongues.

Surround yourself with souls
who nurture your spirit.
Be intentional.
Choose wisely.

Time is a precious gift.
Spend it with those who uplift,
and watch your world bloom.

Lesson in Discomfort

There is a lesson in discomfort.
Your body resists the smallness
of the life you've been living.

Greatness calls you higher.
Can you hear it?

The cognitive dissonance buzzes,
pushing you to action.
Slay the dragons of fear and doubt.
Do what you are afraid to do.

Discomfort is the signal to grow.
Break the chains of comfort.
Navigate the discomfort,
new levels await.

Progress

Progress is calling,
whether from the ashes of old dreams
or the flames of disappointment,
progress is calling you to extinguish
the old and revive the new.
To rise from the ashes.
To place one foot before the other,
walking toward the sun,
with a ferocious appetite for determination
and an unbreakable spirit.
Every setback was a training ground for the child
and the fool within you to mature.
It is the mature who reign,
and the wise who keep their throne
among predators and antagonizers.
It is the chosen who will rule
once they progress past the refining season.

Stillness

The world spins—that is how it was created.
But you are meant to walk forward, backward,
and at necessary times, spin.
If it feels like too much, if it feels chaotic,
you always have the choice to stop spinning.
Pause, listen, breathe.

Beware

Be intentional about your space
and who you invite in.
There are nations within you
and greatness yet to be released.
You are the guardian.
Understand what is best now and for the future.
Choose those you'll do life with, with care.
Time is precious—a treasure most don't realize is rare.

Seek out souls who lift you to greater heights,
and seek no pleasure in weighing you down.
Surround yourself with those who kindle your inner light.
Those who inspire, encourage, and pray
for your truest self to overflow and break the mold.

Be so aware that toxic tendrils have no space
to attach themselves to you or the things you value.
Keep your heart surrendered and serene.
Release the vampire ties that drain you.

Surround yourself with true kindred spirits,
whose love and warmth feel ever-renewing.
The ones who see your worth, celebrate you,
and stand beside you in both storm and fate.

Exactly Enough

You are not too much
awake to your true value
you are exactly enough.

Life's a Journey

Life is a journey we all must take.
No matter our color, culture, or values,
we all arrive through the same canal of our mothers.
We, the survivors, are fortunate enough to
experience twists, turns, and even missteps
we label as mistakes.

But with each step, we have the choice
to learn and grow.
If we're brave and wise enough to lean into the twists
and turns and value the missteps,
we are sure to find beauty in the unknown.

Renewed Wings

Clipped and left wounded,
you didn't know that you could fly.
Beautiful bird, you fell from your nest,
stretching your wings to regain your grip.
It wasn't until this very moment
you learned that you had wings.

With renewed faith and identity,
you spread your wings, ready to fly.
With a resilient spirit, you soar into the open sky.
Higher and higher, you repeatedly glide,
testing your belief that no storm can break you and
no wind could sway you from your course.

God Exists

Mountains rise, we climb
valleys come to test our muscle
each location god exists.

Starting Over

Do you understand how brave you are?
Trying again does not make you a failure.
Trying again is proof to you
and all those around you
that you are powerful and
strong enough to start over.

The Truth

You will never meet the truth in crowds of chaos.
You will not find it in the cheers of the crowd
or tucked away in the bleachers.
It is found in the stillness of the morning,
within the quietest of moments.
There, the deepest truth is unearthed before us.

Grief

Grief does not adhere to a statute of limitations.
It does not ask for your permission to come in.
It enters and rearranges every emotion,
thought and space.
Grief reveals the process of adaptation.
It teaches you how to bare-knuckle it,
fight and heal through it.
Grief teaches us to keep going.

Thoughts

60,000 to 80,000 thoughts pass through
our minds each day.
Some like freight trains, quickly passing by.
Some gentle, some loud, some healing and some painful.
60,000 whispers echo through your mind.
Where your mind goes, your life will also follow.

Harness your positive thoughts.
Lasso the negative,
for your life is a reflection of your thoughts.
You have the power and the choice
to make each one beautiful.

New Light

The sun must adieu
remember dawn will come
keep faith in the new light.

Accepted and Adored

You are completely accepted and adored.
God is not defined by your perceptions
or past disappointments.

He desired you before your body took form.
He desired you before your mama's belly incubated you.
Allow his love to engulf you.
To choose you and restore you.
To be filled with his endless grace.

Purification

The Decree

Hard times transform
from hysterical winds
to piercing raindrops,
each a sharp reminder.
Yet, in the face of calamity
let your decree be this:
"I stand firm upon my solid foundation,
deeply rooted in resilience.
I draw strength from the battles won,
and even the ones lost.
I rise,
I conquer,
I thrive."

Stillness

In the quiet warmth of solitude,
where silence reigns pure,
I build my sanctuary.
A sacred refuge from the noise.

This is where my soul breathes,
where I release the grief I've held.

In the twilight hours, before the world stirs,
I let my heart utter its prayers.
Stillness is a gift,
a balm that heals and restores.

In this sacred silence,
I rediscover myself.

Surrender

In the stillness of this place,
I consecrate this space.

In surrender, I release perfection,
abandoning control
to embrace the ease of divine guidance.

No longer toiling aimlessly,
I trust that my steps are ordered.
With open palms and an open heart,
I find peace.
Letting go of my will
and embracing the wisdom of God.

Power of Forgiveness

Forgiveness is a balm,
healing the hidden and exposed wounds,
a pathway to peace that surpasses understanding.

It reclaims your power,
your freedom,
your light.
Through forgiveness,
you release offense,
allowing your heart to grow.

It's a sacred act:
setting yourself free
from the chains of the past,
transforming wounds into wisdom.

Blossoms Amidst Ruin

Amidst the ruins of deferred dreams,
amidst the rubble of pain,
you were always planting seeds.

Through tears, through gratitude,
through silent endurance,
you sowed the soil of your now.

Blossoms of hope rise,
defying life's strain.
In devastation, seeds grow,
leading to the fire of your destiny.

Not all fires consume;
some purify.

Through resilience and faith,
beauty emerges bold,
heeding God's call
to unfold.

The Alchemy

Life is a masterpiece,
crafted in hardship's forge.
Adversity is useful.
A tool to hone your soul.

Pain is transmuted into gold,
devastation into stories,
stories into roads
that lead others home.

Eyes on the goal,
visualize the finish line.
Fire doesn't destroy you;
it creates you.

The alchemy of life is this:
from ash and flame,
we rise into something more powerful
than we ever imagined.

Peace

With every stone of chaos hurled,
I've gathered and built.

Stone by stone, pain by pain,
I've crafted a dwelling place,
a fortress of peace.

I'm not where you left me;
I'm not who I once was.

Through the art of stillness,
I release what no longer serves me.
I surrender,
fortifying my foundation
with compassion and understanding.

In peace's embrace,
I reside.
A tranquil haven
where serenity abides.

Famine

Your mind is stuck, and your heart lives in famine,
a hunger rooted deep within.
Longing for substance where loneliness has set in.
In the depths of your hunger, your spirit feels drained.

The heart craves nourishment, food for your soul,
not empty or vain, but true sustenance,
meant to keep it whole.

Your spirit starves for its true nature to be found.
Your heart beats and cries out:
How much longer will you let it long for nourishment,
when you can end this famine?

Seek the sustenance within.
It will allow you to hear the quiet whispers of change.
Feed your spirit with its true fruit:
love, joy, peace, patience, kindness,
goodness, faithfulness, and self-control.

Sugar Coated Egos

It's in the way you stand, puffed up,
and the way your tongue slithers
and hisses as you breathe.

Your candy-coated egos are wrapped in toxic sugar,
glossed with transparent shells,
fragile enough to crack with a word,
a look, a boundary,
or a deep exhale that blows too hard.

We see you.
Beneath the meticulous shimmer lies brittleness,
fragility hidden in plain sight.

Renewal

The ashes fool those who lack clarity and wisdom,
leading them to believe that endings
define who you are.

Yet it is within the ending that new cycles of life begin.
Within you lies the promise of new seasons
for your resilient spirit.

Separate, renew, and grow.
When you reach maturity,
there will be a rebirth.

Canvas

If life is a canvas, we are all artists holding the brush,
longing to courageously paint strokes of pain
with colors of joy and shades of love.

Hold your brush and create your masterpiece.
Let your voice be heard,
and your spirit shine bright.

Paint boldly. Paint wide. Paint free,
unafraid of mistakes or the opinions of others.
After all, this is your canvas.

There is plenty for them to judge
if only they had the courage
to fill life's canvas too.

How to Move

You don't need their applause to validate your dreams.
Move quietly.
Move dangerously, but with wisdom.

If you share prematurely,
you risk their tongues of inadequacy
kindling a fire that torches your dreams
and kills your faith.

Be mindful and self-affirming.
Understand that your dreams were placed
within you to be fulfilled with care.

Keep moving.
Rest when you need it.
You are not orphaned.
You are not alone.

You won't make the wrong move.
You just have to move.
You just have to keep going.

New Season

Each season is sure to come.
Some long, cold, and bitter.
Some short, warm, and sweet.
No matter what the harvest brings,
understand that seasons will come and always change.
Like pages in a book, there will be unfolding moments,
a beginning and an ending.
Leave behind the regrets of yesterday,
let your worries fade into the night.
Take rest and bathe in laughter and love,
Just as birds do in overflowing waters.
Embrace your flaws, virtues, quirks and your dreams.
You are a whole being in every way,
and in every season.

Chosen Ones

Cry, let the tears cascade,
For each droplet will be caught, numbered, and bottled.
Each transformed into a testimony of joy.
Life's tempest rages, and burdens grow heavy at times.
Chosen ones, you are handpicked to carry the burden,
for you are strong, pure-hearted, and resolute.

Sustaining the pain, not just for yourself,
but for generations that have yet to come.
Each drop weeps for the bloodline's story,
intricately woven in and out of time,
with each generation graced with resilience.
Crying doesn't make you fragile or weak.

So do not stifle your tears, let them fall,
For each tear speaks of legacy
and how they've overcome.
Each tear holding both wisdom and prayer,
the lineage of those who came before you.

Cry, let the tears cascade,
for tears are the waters that nourish the seeds,
Sown by sacred prayers,
sown for you and the generations yet to be birthed.
All of hell envies you.

Heaven is your home, and you are the apple of my eye.
I am jealous for you.
Do you grasp the truth, the grand facade?
A deceptive ploy, woven to lull you into a slumber.
For you, my beloved, are chosen.

Born of darkness, an embodiment of my essence.
I spoke the words that brought you forth,
molded by my very hands,
formed out of shadows, birthed for a purpose,
a purpose that shines brilliantly as light.

Never believe the lie that you are a mistake,
for I, the Creator, make no errors,
in your being, I have nestled myself,
I gazed upon you with my eyes of love,
my heart pulsates within your very being,
my hands and feet guide your every step,
and you bear the imprint of my divine image.

Envy courses through the depths of hell,
and you, my precious one, the apple of my eye.
A fervent jealousy burns within me,
for I fiercely yearn for your well-being,
I long to see you thrive and flourish,
embracing my purpose for which you were made.

Rise

Fall seven, rise eight
there is power in you
learn and march forward.

Flame

She is a flame, which flickers with an eternal glow,
unapologetically fiery and passionate.
Her very presence graciously illuminates the world,
with ease, she lets her light shine.
She inspires others to ignite,
serving as a pilot for those who need to be reignited.

Born and buried from darkness,
she emerged with clarity of identity,
remnant, chosen one; formed by divine
hands from the depths within,
carrying purpose, she shines as the sun,
for she was born not for darkness, and pain
but for joy, for love, and for the light.

No lie can threaten to dim her fervent blaze,
no venom of deceit could kill her soul's desires.
For she stands on the foundation of truth,
a beacon of authenticity and fierce resolve.

In the envy-filled depths of the abyss,
her light casts shadows that tremble in awe,
she dances with the flames of heaven,
her home is among the stars.

She is an apple of divine affection, cherished and adored,
her essence pulses with a love so pure,
her creator, jealous for her well-being,
guides her through the trials and joys of life.

So let her flame burn ever bright,
an eternal torch of love and might,
igniting hearts, igniting minds,
a blaze that roars through space and time.

Diamond

The blooming diamond
unfolds from the hips of earth,
with clarity and grace.
Your pedigree is cut from royalty.
Your bloom, silent, dark and painful,
withstanding it all for wisdom's sake.
Born to reign for the ones cast aside,
for the dry bones left in the valley to die.
Live again; breathe again.
The cup of bitterness will turn sweet before it ends.
Just tell yourself what has always been true,
this too, shall pass.

Worth

I know my worth; I was tried in the fire,
so every ounce of me is solid gold.
As everything around me depreciates,
I rise in value because my heart, my treasure,
is found in the God who created me in eternity
and placed me into time.

I know my worth; I've been tried in the fire,
given birth to a soul forged with resilience.
I am solid, and every ounce of my being
carries a story, waiting to be told.
As the world around me depreciates and fades,
I rise in value, shining as the light on the hill
that cannot be covered.

The wisdom, peace, and joy are wealth that
cannot be measured, for the connection
to the divine makes my purpose
come alive, through the fire, through the molding.
My character has taken root, and I have become.
Standing tall, I rise in value, strong and bold,
for my worth is not found in material things,
but in love and compassion, what is right
and true, making me a priceless treasure,
yielding seed and producing fruit.

Trailblazer

You walk on roads that turn to gravel, then dirt.
Unpathed paths, where wild grass grows
and it is darker than starless nights.
You're drawn to the blazing mysteries of the unknown,
where sometimes, with light, mysterious creatures
come slithering and prowling by.
Not easily swayed, you are a trailblazer.
With vision and determination, you can't be contained.
You were created to courageously enlarge your borders
and reach into territories of the unknown.
You should know what you do
is not for your satisfaction,
but you'll inspire others to seize the day.

River

Stories of old she holds within.
Taking a few inhales,
I hold the last breath and slowly release
the words and emotions that had lodged themselves
into my psyche, my heart, my nervous system.
I concede—first my toes and then my body.
I let the wisdom of mother river fill my cup.
I need restoration of strength.
How does she do it?
She cuts through rocks instead of moving them.
Instinctually, she turns chaos into rhythm,
and nature creates songs in her honor.
She flows endlessly and graciously,
unfolding to the path carved before her.
She makes friends with uncertainty that flows
from mountains and valleys alike.
She doesn't stop; she doesn't wait.
She flows around, stretched long,
leaning and releasing herself into each twist and turn.
She fine-tunes her strength, and in the evolving, she
doesn't overthink her steps, she just becomes.

Force

You are a force.
Time after time, you have resurrected
from the ashes beautifully unbreakable.
Conquering valleys and humbling mountains
with your cloak of resilience.
You see the world through eyes of faith
and a heart of hope.
Fire and royalty flow through your veins just alike.
You are a force to reckon with.

Grace

With grace and intentionality, she steps,
every step predestined, so she does not focus
on the possibility that she just may stumble.
She is her own sunrise, full of hope and dreams.
She is pure gold.
Her heart, though it is guarded, sometimes takes a lick.
That doesn't stop the magnetic pull;
her heart recalibrates and reorients,
for it is a compass helping her locate true north.

She keeps it clean, but that doesn't mean
it has not felt the shadows.
She masters dancing in the dark
as beautifully as she does in the light.
A pure heart, adorned beneath blue skies,
understanding that even troubled skies
bring blossoms of rainbows.
She has a front-row seat as all creation
sneaks a peek and makes shy glances
towards the one who has made her
to bear his image.

Voices

The external voices will tell you who to be,
how to act, what to wear and how to be happy.
Their voices are loud, let your voice be louder.

Human Spirit

The human spirit is like unto a maze.
Your life's wondering becomes meaningful
as you roam ferociously searching your heart,
unearthing buried truths.
You are the lost desiring to be found.
The deeper you go,
the closer you move toward who
you were predestined to become.

Boldly

Paint your life boldly, and courageously
outside of the lines.
Don't take yourself too seriously.
Life isn't about perfection.
It's about moving and operating
with a spirit of excellence.
You don't have to have it all together.
You're allowed to be a mess
and still deserve everything good.
You're allowed to be a mess and still deserve love.

Pause

What if you saw the ground as a pause,
instead of failure?
Would you still be afraid to fall
or even take a step forward?
Life choices are what build the roads
beneath our very feet.
Step, stumble, wander, and pause.
That's how you learn which way to go.

Comparison

You are not them, and they are not you.
That is the gift.
Each fingerprint, each mind, each spirit
not made in the likeness of others,
But made to stand original to enter,
connect and uphold humanity.
Comparison fades in the light of your authentic self.

Fire

I have never been afraid of fire.
In fact, I played with it over and over,
rolling it between my fingers,
and walking graciously through it
with the understanding that it cannot
burn me because I was forged there.

Patience

Patience is a slow, quiet work
that does not reveal itself externally,
but internally.
Our roots stretch deeper and deeper,
unseen but known by the steady rhythm
of waiting, strengthening.
You and patience becoming one,
so that you may unlock treasures of revelation,
to unlock virtue.

Anomaly

It was only through the moments of outcast
and being pushed into the shadows
that one could discover a kindling of inner glow.
Gentle and warm, your true identity goes undetected,
and your presence is easily unknown.
Overlooked by the untrained eyes,
by the haughty, who are only familiar with the cliché,
the shiny, and the glitz.

The Healing

Healing

In the haven of my soul,
I tend to wounds with gentle care,
Turning to my Father's throne,
where he reveals to redeem.
Embracing the power of healing,
allowing scars, both seen and unseen,
to transform into strength.
With every tear shed, he catches them,
numbers them, and bottles them,
and my heart instinctually mends.
Oh, how you care for even my tears.
I rest under your wings,
to reclaim my spirit, whole and renewed.

The Journey Within

Amidst the chaos,
the self-inflicted wounds
and the pressure,
I persevere.
Collecting what was once obliterated,
piece by piece, my peace, I've found.
Peace, I savor you.
Mindfully inhaling you into my nostrils.
Within the depths of my mind, my heart, my spirit,
I embrace introspection.
Rummaging through my inner jungle,
leaving no stone unturned.
My healing is here, so inward
I journey to depths unknown.
Until the version of who I need
and want to be is revealed.

Self- discovery

Self-discovery releases an incense
only familiar to the profound.
I am boldly embracing the beauty of my being,
and the authenticity of my becoming.
Unveiling the layers of self-love,
nurturing and bathing my soul
with tenderness and mercy.
Loving every inch of this pure heart,
of this crown, and this outer shell.
I am a masterpiece of flaws, dignity,
and strengths, a woman worthy of eternal love.

Emerging

Like a butterfly emerging from its cocoon,
I shake free the layers that once defined me,
embracing the beauty of this healing version of me.
Unfolding my wings to reach new heights.
Unable to return to the small
and constricted places and people who once bound me.
Adventure and purpose await me.
In the freedom of self-expression,
I soar, unlocking levels, releasing the old and
welcoming the new versions of myself.
I embrace truth, wisdom, and love.
I welcome more light.
I welcome more love.
I welcome more authenticity.
I welcome who I was always destined to be.

Gratitude

In the garden of gratitude,
I cultivate seeds of appreciation.
Of all the creations, I was chosen for this point in time.
Not a rock or leaf, but a creature
made of flesh and bones,
in the image of our creator.
Nourishing my soul with thankfulness,
embracing life's blessings, big and small.
With each breath, I release an offering,
and I find solace,
in the abundance that surrounds me.

A Time of Laughter

Her laughter bubbles up and spills over,
watering the very soil she treads,
the overflow floats to the heavens,
creating melodies of joy.
She becomes light and carefree.
The warmth of her laughter sings,
becoming the tempo for all of the creations' songs.
Her infectious joy leaves no heart
untouched or un-warmed.
The beauty of her laughter heals through and through,
And no matter how far you travel,
you'll never be the same.

Perspective

What if it's the lens through which you're viewing life?
Not just by choice, but because life's circumstances have
caused you to view things through a tainted perspective.
Clean your lens, adjust the angle.
Adjust your position with a humble step back,
this may help you see the entire picture clearly.

Pure and Beautiful

I hope that everything that is pure and beautiful
comes into your space and overtakes you,
just as the playful waves overtake the sand
and the sun overtakes the darkness.
I hope all of your dreams come true.
That you remain open-hearted with expectations
of blessings, of the prayers you've sealed with tears.
And when they come to pass,
don't forget the importance of gratitude.
The importance of the one who
gives good and perfect gifts.

The Strength of Foundations

Sinking sand or concrete?
The strength of one's foundation is
only revealed through storms.
Some foundations crumble at the warning of high winds,
others at the beat of the rain and the contact of debris.
Then there are some that sway,
bend, and withstand category five.
What is your foundation built on?
Will the generations now and those who
come after you have the fortitude to stand,
or will they buckle at their knees
because you chose to take the way
that lessened your pain?
The strength of your foundation
will carry the cycles and patterns
to the generations that follow after you.

Growth

She is like a seed in fertile soil,
intentionally stretching her roots to the depths
and width of the earth.
With virtue and authority, she stretches,
reaching for nourishment of life.
Growing, evolving, and embracing change.
With each passing season,
she blooms, she thrives, she becomes.
Becomes more than what she was told she could ever be.
She becomes more than what she needed to prove.
She becomes the mighty tree planted by the water,
blooming in season and out.

Be Well

If your journey provokes them
and your growth offends them,
Remember, you are but a mirror
exposing what cannot be hidden.

You cannot betray yourself and halt your process,
just to appease the boundaries of their approval.
Your evolution and necessity,
knows no limits set by the permission of others.

If this renewed and healing version of yourself
causes true offense within their being,
gently remind them that love and healing
won't hold anyone hostage.
A mutual release is necessary.
Be free.
Just as Job released the blessing to his friends
send them genuine blessings.
Pack for them love and light,
to embrace on their own unique journey.
Close the door and do not look back.

Strength

Strength blooms in silence
in the storm, she finds her fire
grace forged by her fight.

Self-love

No need to shout at yourself.
Speak softly and gently,
hold yourself in highest regard.
You don't need spas, facials, external validation.
What you need is time for yourself
and self-compassion.

The Healing Woman

To the woman quietly healing within,
I offer you a note of grace.
I offer you love and light.

You've weathered storms,
sometimes anxious and afraid,
wondering if you'll drown in tears
that seem to have no end.

Don't focus on the process.
Don't focus on the pain.
You're learning to fly at higher altitudes
through every season.

Sometimes burdened, brought to your knees,
you are more powerful than you think.
Congratulations, you didn't concede to the pain.
Keep healing; your soul is calling you to rise again.

In your depths, you hold the power
to mend wounds and transmute pain into purpose.
Let your hands trace the scars that map your story,
a tribute to strength and a precursor of glory.
Remember the scars.

Coronation Season

You've walked through the belly of the beastly fire,
not consumed or devoured,
but emerging with light.

Taking flight, making the phoenix bow
to your divine daughtership.
Healing woman, you were made low
only for a moment,
so you could soar like the eagle.

Unleash your spirit.
This is the time you were created for.

Release every burden,
and let forgiveness sweep through your temple.
Lean into healing, replenishing your spirit day by day.

Nurture your soul with kindness and care,
for self-love is the seed you bear.

Embrace the journey,
both highs and lows.
For each altitude brings wisdom that grows.
You are resilient, brave, and strong.
Healing woman, you are as whole
as you allow yourself to be.

Rise, healing woman.
New heights are calling.

The Heart of a Fighter

The heart of a fighter
is one that endures life's whirls
and sucker punches.

Mighty and fierce,
through hardships obscure,
we rise up, standing tall.

Through every challenge, we find a way.
Though fiery darts pursue,
the fighter's heart conquers all.

With our path steady and spirit strong,
we stand our ground, enduring the dark,
shining through it all.

With determination and grit,
we mount up wings like eagles.
We persevere.
We never quit.

A Father's Love

God built you with His gentle, steady hands.
Over you, he sang the notes of a father in love
with the image that lay before Him.

He breathed life into your nostrils,
jealous for you, reaching for your hand,
guiding your footsteps.

He assigns his angels to protect you,
even when you stray beyond the boundaries.
His words thunder; His anger unmatched
when predators threaten to devour and overtake you.

He loves you.
He is your Father.

When you are ready,
reach out and grab his hand.

Mending

Within the walls of my soul,
I tend to the wounds with gentle care,
I turn into my Father's throne,
where he reveals to redeem,
embracing the power of healing,
allowing scars to transform into strength.
With every tear shed, he catches them
and places them in a bottle.
He numbers each tear.
Even the ones I bitterly swallowed are accounted for.
Yet, with His presence, my heart mends.
How it breaks, scars, wounds, yet instinctually mends.
My mind could never comprehend.
I just know in this moment, I reclaim my spirit,
whole and renewed,
ready to continue moving and flowing in purpose.

Light Bearer

It is through the absence of light that
we comprehend our existence.
You carry light in your soul.
With each step forward,
you illuminate the way.
Forward, forward, walk yourself forward.
Your power lies ahead,
You have no reason to turn back.
Catch a glimpse of your reflection,
In the placid puddles.
In your presence, shadows quake
with terror and fade.
Each step leads you closer to hope,
and soon, it will all make sense.

Faith

This is your gentle reminder
that faith does not lie within the knowing.
It is trusting, even when your eyes and mind
cannot see the next step.

Empowered

Her mind is a fortress, built on the foundation of wisdom
reinforced with walls of unapologetic boldness.
She is an empowered woman, with stories untold.
With a crown of knowledge and insight,
she breaks the mold,
mentally and spiritually empowered, a force to behold.

Her body, a temple, strong and fierce,
an empowered woman, through fears she perseveres.
With her heart ablaze with passion and love,
she spreads love, compassion, and empathy.

Emotionally empowered,
her spirit, radiant and bright,
she's leaning in and embracing her light.
With connection and purpose, she rises.

In mind, body, heart, and spirit,
she embraces her power, her given purpose defined.
An empowered woman,
her strength made known in presence.
Mentally, physically, emotionally, spiritually aligned.

Mastering Letting Go

Letting go is an art,
that even the mastery of artists has met with difficulties.
Sometimes, stuck in the psyche,
unable to manifest on canvas.
Even with habitual permission
and hands lifted in surrender,
our hearts cling so tightly
to the pain that we have known,
often forgetting that in our desperate grip,
in bondage, we cannot truly grow.
So that the creativity of our canvas can be free,
we must learn the art of saying no more,
and letting go of all that holds us down.
Trust that in the freedom gained,
we are free to rise, glide, and soar.
Putting down the things we carry
will make room for our joy and blessings to be found.

Dreams

Fear will scream and rage,
it believes that if it screams loud enough,
it will shatter your dreams.
But your dreams are not fragile;
they wait quietly and obediently
for you to believe in the ferocity of them.

Exposure

When you had the choice to remain covered and dry,
you saw me drenched with rain.
You abandoned safety so that I was assured
that I was never alone.
You understood me, and I saw the
handsomeness of your soul.
The gift of your presence,
the gift of this moment,
I'll always remember.

Passion

Our passion will fade
when we neglect refueling.
Rest and recover.
It is the only way we are able to
fortify what others try to tear down.

You Can

You can choose to give up, but that's not where life ends.
What if it's hard because you were created for influence?
Within the pain lies purpose, an honorable privilege.
What if you're almost to the other side?
If you crossover, you'll see that you have the power
to shape lives and set hearts free.
To inspire change and water the roses
growing through concrete.
The kindest of hearts must learn that
self-preservation and self-love
must be a lifelong art.
Establishing boundaries, healthy and strong.
Holding them firmly with pure intentions,
even when tantrums and disrespect threaten
to storm the castle.
Protect your spirit from evil agendas,
respecting yourself and others too.

Fill Your Cup

You've filled the cups of others,
poured and poured until you've emptied
your soul into everyone else.
You've stretched yourself and stretched some more,
you've stretched yourself thin.
Who carries you when your cup is empty,
who carries you when you're buckling under the weight?
Who has keen enough hearing to hear the faint cries
of your exhaustion?
Pour what you need first.
Pour love, self-compassion,
pour kindness and grace until your cup spills over.
Fill your cup with love and joy.
Let it overflow until it touches lives,
opens hearts, and unlocks doors of mentality.

The Beauty of Change

There is beauty in understanding that all things change.
They die and come alive when they're buried
in darkness and preserved in good soil.
Things change depending on how we water them,
where we plant them, how we prune them
and cut back the weeds
that try to choke the life out of them.
What if we lived more intentionally
with the understanding that what is here,
and in this moment, can instantly cease to exist.
Whether it be tangible or intangible,
whether it be good or bad,
everything changes in an instant.

Choose

Learn to choose people who choose you,
surround yourself with those who truly see you.
Seek those connections where you truly feel loved
because it flows unconditionally
from pure heart to pure heart.
Do not be afraid, you will not be consumed.
For there is a fire that true authentic souls have,
a heat that will scourge everything that is false.
Do not settle for less than you deserve,
this is the season to hold your power of self-respect
and worth at greatest esteem.
Choose mutual respect and support
select your circle with wisdom,
and you will find rare and genuine bonds
that will place you at destiny's table.

Freedom

Freedom is not the ability to escape mentally,
to compartmentalize or run away.
True freedom is being aware of it all,
yet you stand still, trenches dug,
and you choose yourself over and over again.

Only a Lesson

In failure, we find that there really aren't any failures,
only wrong turns in order to discover new lands,
only lessons learned to create and train your hand
to be steady for the war against destiny thieves.
Thieves that have studied from ancient wolves
from scheming serpents that appear
solely to squeeze life from your purpose.
Do not drink from the cup of shame and bitterness,
do not eat from the plate of anger.
There is no dishonor in missing the goals you've created
in your conditioned and caged mind.
Make the wrong turns, go up a mile,
and wisdom is straight ahead.
Stumble backwards and stagger off course,
peace is to your left.
It is in discomfort that one grows
and stretches out their border.
It is within the territory of perceived failure
that we strike gold and find great success.

Legacy

From roots deep down, a legacy grows.
A family's love intricately sown,
through time and generations,
a dynasty stands tall.
Each elder stands like regal and glorious
ancient oak trees.
Wise and grand, they are pillars who stand on
the shoulders of the ancestors that came before.
Heirs to the kingdom, they carve with a steady hand.
With our whispers of wisdom,
our young one will grow.
Teach their pinkies to war and their hands to be steady.
Teach them to uphold family values.
The stories that run through their bloodline
and the power that holds them together,
to carry their dreams and legacy to distant lands.

Connection

We are designed for connection,
even the most introverted among us.
We don't need a room full of people,
just a few selected, or one,
that hear the words when we cannot speak.

Humility

Humility isn't dimming your light,
nor is it shrinking yourself down
to an unnatural state.
It is pointing your crown upward,
without having the biggest or flashiest.
It is standing tall without having to be
the tallest in the room.
It is having the strength, yet not needing
to show how strong you are.
It is understanding your worth
without shouting it aloud and allowing
a space for others to shine in their worth.

Incredible Rebirth

Isn't it incredible how one can blossom amidst ruins.
How one can burn down
and transform from rubble and ashes.
How we rise from the soil in obedience to God's voice.
Isn't it beautiful that from the soil,
from the ashes, destiny emerges,
and chosen kings and queens rise,
strong, powerful, and bold.

Gentleness

Be gentle with yourself and with others,
Some appear to be shallower than meets the eye.
Some, you will never know their depth
until you're submerged, searching for a lifesaver.
Have firm boundaries and remember
be gentle with yourself and gentle with others.
Remember, time could never heal
what is not worked on, nor
what you are not made aware of.
What is not cleaned and treated with love
and compassion, only festers.
Be gentle with yourself
and be gentle with others.

In Your Presence

In Your closeness,
I'm learning to find my purpose,
I'm commanding my heart to beat
to the cadence of your love and glory,
to dance with true joy and gratitude.
Your creations surround me
and your grace tenderly embraces me.
In your presence, I feel safe;
I am certain that I am secure.
I feel fulfilled and whole.
I am revived, purified, and renewed.
Every step of my journey,
you endure.
I am never alone.

The Crowning

The Coronation

In the stillness of the morning, she rises,
before dawn breaks, she fixes her gaze
and commands her day.
Planning each move,
she steps into the arena of life.

She stands tall,
her shoulders squared, and
eyes fixed ahead.
Knowingly, she gazes out and ahead.

The journey has been long and strenuous,
marked by trying times.
Preparation tethered with perseverance,
challenges that shape the soul,
and yet, here she stands,
as if she was never gracefully broken,
she stands affirmed, sure and complete.

In the quiet of this moment,
she can feel the weight of destiny,
a purpose that courses through her veins,
a calling that echoes her heart,
pushing her forward.

As the sun rises, casting its golden light,
this is her crowning;
the celebration of her survival,
a celebration of her elevation.
This is the moment of coronation.

Coronation Season

Not with jewels or throne,
but with purpose, pure and true,
with love, and recognition of all she's endured,
and all she's become.

In this moment, she is royalty,
not by birthright, but by virtue,
by the strength of her spirit,
by the depth of her compassion,
by the love that courses through her.

And as she raises her head to the sky,
she knows that this is only the beginning,
for with purpose, and with love,
she is crowned

as a queen,
in her own right.

Seasons Change

In every season, she is in full bloom,
a luminescent light that eradicates gloom.
From the freshness of spring,
to the vibrant summer songs,
within autumn's warm shades and winter's night long.
She unfolds, and unearths her full potential.
Her mind and her soul are exponential.
In every season, her beauty stays true,
she is timeless, a wonder the world can view.

The Weight of the Crown

Just because I carry it with grace
doesn't mean it isn't heavy,
This crown of strength, truth and authority
both brilliantly bright and steady.
I wear it high, with dignity and honor,
yet hidden burdens I cannot truly hide.

Being "the strong one", the chosen one,
means bearing weight unseen,
a weight that I don't bear entirely alone,
the presence of my angels is known.

But a silent struggle only I, and kindred spirits hold
the blueprint of the generational promises.
Nature whispers what I know but often forfeit,
I can be strong and cry tears of vulnerability,
for even warriors, kings and queens become wounded
yes, even those with pure hearts bleed.

Eternal Seeds of Resilience

In fertile soil I was sown,
through darkness and depth my soul took root.
Though storms tantrum and rage on
although it seeks to destroy me,
I won't be frightened; I will not be moved.
I rise each day,
understanding the divine protection that surrounds me.
So come what may, howling winds
seeking to intimidate and bend me
but resiliency is my spirit's diadem.
Grow and thrive is what I set my intentions on.

Leaving to Receive

Dear giver, this is your time to receive.
Open your hands, open your heart
to harvest all that you have sown.
Always pouring into others, always there.
Sit back and let others wash your feet.
Let yourself receive freely each gift
offered without condition.

King and Queens Flight

From ashes beauty was born.
In place of your tattered and torn spirit
a liveliness has taken flight and your spirit now soars.
Through battle fatigue and the stench of defeat
our spirit and soul endure.
With my crown to the sky
and heart prostrate in surrender,
We rise above until we are set to endure.
My will intertwined with my Abba.
So, I can endure the heat, discomfort and pain.
Knowing that through the comfortability
growth can begin.
New territories and authority are released,
as my tests are marked complete
and turned to testaments.
Through our fiery trials, we become beautifully refined,
the scars we bear serve as a testimony
of how we became free,
and how we became crowned king and queen.

Crown of Beauty

Spun pain into gold,
he, the alchemist of words,
melted it down,
forming a crown of authority.

With each breath,
he called forth his finest stones,
diamonds and rubies,
he sent angels to scourer the depths of his treasury.

With each breath he called forth
his angels to wash me in the blood of his son.
From each strand of hair to each groove on my feet
his love and sacrifice seal me.

No good thing did he withhold,
sparing no precious gem,
joint heir he anointed and titled me,
adorning me in the presence,
of all spiritual beings.

Coronation Season

Completing my coronation,
he sealed me in kiros,
the essence of divine time,
and knit me together and placed me in chronos.
He gave me his Spirit.
Reminding me that I am never forsaken,
he is with me always and in all ways.

Because in his artistry,
he saw beauty in brokenness,
transforming my scars,
into a regal testament of strength.
He is my Abba, and I am his crown of beauty.

Noble Character

You who are of noble character, stand tall,
crowns of integrity lifted to the sky.

You strive to embody virtues, never to deceive.
With integrity as your compass,
this is your time of great honor.

Arise now; stand tall and true.
With honesty and compassion as your shield,
let truth and your values be your sword.

May your path be illuminated always,
guiding you forward as you journey on.

A Queen's King

I looked to my left and smiled,
you smiled back.
It was the moment a million
possibilities were born.
It was the moment that my love found its home.
My heart vowed that she needed your
heart to wrap its arm around her.
To stay for eternity and love her outside of time.
I just didn't know it until now.

Wisdom

The pressure, it squeezes as life tosses you
back and forth, up and down.
Lessons they cut your achilles, causing pain and blood
the survivor in you crawls toward the light.
"No, stop, you'll heal if you stay still, don't fight".
The onlookers and self- doubt will shout.
But if you stay still time won't heal you,
you'll slowly bleed out.
Crawl through the pain,
move through the hardship.
You'll never receive wisdom at the beginning of a lesson.
You get the hurt, the denial, you feel the discomfort.
Wisdom waits for you at the end,
she meets you at the finish line.
You must move forward,
you must move through to collect her,
as one collects a badge of honor.

Determination

Are your eyes steady?
Fix your sight on what you want,
even when fear challenges your stance,
move toward it with your whole heart and being.
One step at a time,
one smaller goal at a time.
The journey has to shape you,
it has to strengthen your
might and teach you.
Don't waste your steps,
make each one worth it.

Will You?

I am the garden; will you tend to me?
Will you water me?
Do you have the courage to pull back the aged curtains
and force the darkness out of hiding?
Will you teach me to let the sun in.
Will you remove the snakes and provide divine order?

Boundless Visionary

The visionary fixes their eyes on the horizon.
To the one who lacks, there is nothing.
But the visionary sees what is beyond.
Borders do not exist; their mind unfolds like ancient maps storing secret treasures to behold.
No limits, just territories waiting to be discovered and vaulted mysteries to be unlocked.
Even with societal pressures, the visionary maneuvers from their grasp.
They refuse to be confined by conditions or limitations.
Their mind only sees possibilities,
and their potential is destined to reach beyond the galaxies and touch the feet of heaven.

You

The warmth of your smile
vibrates through me chasing shades
of blue away from me.

Messy Grace

Life is messy,
there isn't always
a direct path to where you
are and where you want to be.
Rest assured, within every muddled step,
there is grace.

Hero

Be the hero in your own story,
the one who falls but embraces the pause,
the one who chooses to rise,
who overcomes and finds strength and courage
when met with every challenge.
Not because you're so amazing
or because it's easy, but
because you've learned to
bandage the scrapes and rise even when it's hard.

Strength Applauded

The world sees the smiles,
but inside, so many storms of fear,
anger, and sadness rage unbound.
Both silent and resilient.
Your strength I applaud.

Perfect Pace

Your pace is perfect
don't you dare rush perfection
to be accepted.

Simplicity

Sometimes, enough is right here.
You overthink it and complicate
out of self-doubt.
Haven't you risen from doubt before?
There is no need to search for a strength
you've proven time and time again.
Not everything needs to be more,
it just requires you to walk it out.

Free

Let the wild in you breathe,
whisper into her heart the wisdom
of boundaries, then let her run free,
the world needs your untamed zeal,
a spark to set other fearful souls free.
So, clothe yourself with confidence,
and run, run, run free.

Letting Yourself Feel It

You do not have to be strong all the time.
I know, if you don't, who will, right?
Wrong, you'll crumble and break with this mindset.
Feel it, all of it.
Feel the anger, feel the sadness,
feel the worry and feel the joy.
Feel it all.
There is power in your humanness,
to be fragile and strong,
to feel everything so deeply,
yet keep holding on.
You're just as powerful when you cry as when you laugh.
I give you permission to give yourself permission
to feel it all.

Imperfections

The right hearts will always meet you where you're at.
They will see you with all your imperfections
and choose you and the flaws.
You do not have to be someone else
to be loved and valued.

Energy

What feeds you?
What makes you feel alive?
Save your energy and your
time for that.
Wisdom is knowing and understanding
that not everything deserves your energy.

Coronation Season

Calm

In the storm's winds,
through each season's change,
we find the calm in our core.

The Gift

Your presence is a gift.
You should always protect it
so your worth never shrinks.

Queen's Play

Never be the loudest in the room,
sit back and watch how the players move.
A queen must stand firmly planted in this game of life.
With her mind as steady as her crown.
10 steps ahead, strategic paths waiting to be tread.
She moves, shifts, and sways through battles,
carefully considering the risks.
Mistakes are high, but not as high as
if she doesn't take the risk.
Kings rise and fall, pawns become disqualified,
but the queen holds power both inside and out.
She is fit to reign.
For she knows when to rise
and sacrifice to secure the win.

Wealth Within

If you look for the glitter and gold,
the jewels you can hold in hand,
or ornament your neck and wrist,
you miss true worth
and settle for fool's gold.
Those things will shine and tarnish.
They will appreciate and depreciate.
True wealth lies within the purest of hearts,
the kindest of hands, and the one with a peaceable
mind, soul, and spirit.
It is found in the pursuit of dreams
and the welcoming of joy.
It is in gratitude for all those who have come and gone.
For those who stay and see you.
It is in the freedom of taking the unpopular path.
It is not in the tangible, but the priceless things.
It is in family and friends and all the
love you choose to give.

To Heal

It won't always be like this.
Your life can be a mess, yet you'll survive
and thrive when you learn to train your mind.
Let gratitude fill the room,
even if crying decides to accompany you.
Your purpose requires you to be mentally strong.
There is a power that healing will release from you.
You've weathered the storms and
flourished through the drought.
Your wounds have scarred, a map for your testimony.

You've walked through the belly of the beastly fire,
not devoured, but becoming the devourer
and emerging with light.
For just a moment, you were made lowly,
so you could rise to your greatest height.
It was not by accident,
it is a necessary readjustment to your course.

Everyone can't go, they'll suffocate at this new level.
This is the time of your rebirth.
Release every burden,
and let forgiveness sweep your temple clean.
Lean into the healing, do not fight.
Welcome the highs and the lows,
for you are resilient and whole.
With every step forward, grow in wisdom
and rise with strength, for new heights are calling
and it's destined to make you uncomfortable.

Such a Time as This

You were created for such a time as this
to love and be loved.
You were created to reflect light,
even when they try to dim your brilliance.
You are protected and surrounded by the eternal flame.
You had to be hard-pressed,
it strengthens the soil.
You grow wider when you are pruned.
Who taught you that the pressure would consume you,
isn't pressure how gems bloom
and the favor is produced?
Aren't there contractions before birth
and storms before blessings?
Cry your last tear, this season has been completed.
Clean your face and straighten your back.
The tears were your bread and water so you
would know the difference between sorrow and joy.
Hold your head high,
you were created for such a time as this.
This is the moment that you are being crowned.

Empathy

Never underestimate the empathy that blooms
in the heart of the one who is pure and true.
They understand how to unfold with limited to no light.
The muck and mire water their buds of understanding.
They live between two worlds,
where deep and unsearchable things can be found.
They have been tested and have been found worthy.

Remember Who You Are

When they come and barter for the price
of your self-worth, remember who you are.
Remember the resistance and the unraveling,
remember the fire and the pain it took
for you to arrive here and now.
Understand that they would only barter if they didn't
see how valuable you truly are.
Raise your price and become more exclusive.
Those who value you won't want
you at a discounted price.
Those who value you will empathize
with how much surrendering and sacrifice
it took for you to become who stands
before them now.

Mirror, Mirror

Mirror, mirror on the wall,
peel back the layers, the masks worn by all.
Let all pretense and façade disintegrate
until only the raw and unguarded truth is left.
Stand brave and vulnerable, risking full transparency.
In a world where illusions feast on delusions
causing truth to die, keep a guarded and open heart.
Do not mimic; let your voice pierce true.
Be unfaltering with genuineness and integrity.
Stand your ground unapologetic and unveiled.
For this is where the soul thrives
and all the good will meet you unmasked, bare.

Unshaken

She stands, unshaken
a voice unbroken, steady
ready to trumpet.

Qualities

Your qualities are unlike any other,
you are truly a gem, fully your own.
You'll never fit in, designed to stand out,
to think differently, to lead lost souls
to their original home.
Your uniqueness is your strength,
created to be heard, to be seen,
to be an agitator for anything untrue.
Embrace yourself,
because you'll live eternity with you.

Create

She holds the pen and has
the power to harness thoughts.
She wields her pen like a knight holding a sword.
Ink flows and bends at her will, alchemist.
She is turning words into gold as her thoughts
rope the lines of the pages
and perform as though stages were made
just for its amusement.
Words move forward with clarity.
She holds her pen, and creativity bows.
A storyteller, inspiring hearts with each written line.

Unfinished Dreams

Some wait silently in the shadows.
No stars to light its way.
Half-lived, half-completed tasks
waiting to be revived.
It's okay to ignite the passions again,
to breathe new life and start again.
Some dreams are crafted at the wrong moments.
Some need maturity.
Rework the vision and begin again.

The Courage to Crossover

Crossing over is scary,
you are leaving the familiar,
people, places, and things behind.

Clothed in Strength

She is clothed in strength, carrying a flame
of eternity sacredly connected to the divine.
Her presence commands respect
and her words are filled with self-worth.
She embraces each moment as it unfolds before her eyes.
In her is dominion, she holds power and grace,
to speak to all creation, a reflection of love and devotion.

Seasons Change

I used to laugh to keep from crying,
now I laugh because happiness rises
and laughter gleefully spills from my lips.
I choose joy, happiness, and celebration
for the promise that all seasons change.
A celebration for all that I am
and the billions of possibilities that
are yet to become.

The Fruit of Possibilities

When you stand before the mirror,
I hope your eyes do not see
your reflection smiling back.
I hope you instead see the infinite possibilities
flowering, ready for you to delve in
and pick from its ripe tree.

Simply Being

There is so much peace in simply being.
You were never meant to toil
and wander around aimlessly.
Fine-tune your sight.
Practice intentional stillness.
Set yourself free from the cage of others' expectations,
join the wild ones, refuse to be controlled.
Sit with your creator, the blueprint is in his hands.
There are rooms you were created for,
there are communities that you were fashioned to save.
There are hardened hearts that will melt
like wax at the sound of your voice.
But it requires you to be content in stillness.

Battlefield

In life's battlefield, she fights with love,
she is unlike other warriors.
She doesn't use anger and pain as her shield.
She is a warrior of compassion, that is her armor.
Her heart is her shield and her truth and kindness
are her piercing swords.
She conquers and subdues by spreading love,
and she slays dragons of fear,
through healing, and self-awareness.
She is a fierce and unstoppable warrior.
Training others to fight and hold the line
of defense and offense alike.

Symphony

In our harmony, do you feel it?
Can you hear it?
Your very own symphony, heaven and earth aligned,
balancing the notes of mind, body, and spirit.
Melodies of inner peace play on
as you dance under the stars with self-love and care.
As the music plays, move to the rhythm of the tempo.
This is it.
You are becoming.

You Are Still Becoming

Be gentle with yourself,
you don't have to have it all figured out.
Healing and growth will always take root
in the space with the least resistance.
Release your timeline, there is no perfect timing.
The cracks are not for sanding and painting over,
the light cannot consume the hidden places,
it cannot wash the darkness away.
You don't need to apologize for taking your time,
you don't have to explain your process.
While you are becoming, you're being refined
and you are allowed to rest.
Resting is not quitting; it is a refueling.
Release the guilt, you are not lazy, just human.
Gather your strength for what is up ahead.
Trust that even your small, shaky steps are important.
Trust that the person that you are becoming
is waiting at the finish line and they are
already proud of you.

Dear Reader,

You are not where you are by accident. Every step of your journey, every joy, pain, setback, and victory has shaped you for a purpose that only you can fulfill. This book ends here, but your story continues. Even in moments of uncertainty, within you lies the strength, courage and grace to rise to the occasion.

You are chosen. You are equipped. You are enough. You were created to shine "for such a time as this."

With love and encouragement,
Lakeya Brown

www.ingramcontent.com/pod-product-compliance
Lightning Source LLC
Chambersburg PA
CBHW050224100526
44585CB00017BA/1942